SACRAN S0-DUS-537

Sacramento, CA 95814
09/20

The Life and Times of

PETER STUYVESANT

Mitchell Lane
PUBLISHERS

P.O. Box 196 · Hockessin, Delaware 19707

Titles in the Series

The Life and Times of

PETER STUYVESANT

Jim Whiting

Copyright © 2008 by Mitchell Lane Publishers, Inc. All rights reserved. No part of this book may be reproduced without written permission from the publisher. Printed and bound in the United States of America.

Printing　　1　　2　　3　　4　　5　　6　　7　　8　　9

Whiting, Jim, 1943–
The life and times of Peter Stuyvesant / by Jim Whiting.
　　p. cm.— (Profiles in American history)
　Includes bibliographical references and index.
　ISBN 978-1-58415-526-3 (library bound)
　1. Stuyvesant, Peter, 1592–1672—Juvenile literature. 2. Governors—New York (State)—Biography—Juvenile literature. 3. New York (State)—History—Colonial period, ca. 1600–1775—Biography—Juvenile literature. 4. New Netherland—Biography—Juvenile literature. I. Title.
　F122.1.S78W48 2008
　974.7'02092—dc22
　[B]
　　　　　　　　　　　　　　　　　　　　　　　　　　　　2007023196

ABOUT THE AUTHOR: Jim Whiting has been a remarkably versatile and accomplished journalist, writer, editor, and photographer for more than 30 years. A voracious reader since early childhood, Mr. Whiting has written and edited more than 250 nonfiction children's books on a wide range of topics. He lives in Washington state with his wife and two teenage sons.

PHOTO CREDITS: Cover, pp. 1, 3—Library of Congress; pp. 6, 12—Barbara Marvis; p. 11—Old Galleries; p. 16—Peter Schenk; p. 17—Jack Dodge; p. 18—John Collier; pp. 21, 22, 26, 36, 39—North Wind Picture Achives; p. 24—Howard Pyle; p. 28—Peter Spier; p. 32—Jonathan Scott

PUBLISHER'S NOTE: This story is based on the author's extensive research, which he believes to be accurate. Documentation of such research is on page 46.

　　The internet sites referenced herein were active as of the publication date. Due to the fleeting nature of some web sites, we cannot guarantee they will all be active when you are reading this book.
　　　　　　　　　　　　　　　　　　　　　　　　　　　　　　　　　PLB

Profiles in American History

Contents

A statue of Peter Stuyvesant stands in Stuyvesant Square, land in present-day New York City that once was part of his farm. The statue, erected in 1941, shows his wooden leg, the result of a battle wound.

CHAPTER 1

The Man with the Wooden Leg

Sometime in March 1644, Peter Stuyvesant landed on St. Martin, an island in the Caribbean Sea. He was leading a Dutch expedition to recapture the island. Settlers of the Dutch West India Company had occupied St. Martin in 1631, but the Spanish had taken control two years later.

The Dutch wanted St. Martin back. Stuyvesant was told that the fort protecting the island was lightly garrisoned, with only a handful of Spanish soldiers. He thought he could retake St. Martin without much trouble. Maybe the Spanish soldiers would even surrender without a fight.

At the time, Stuyvesant was the governor of the Dutch-controlled Caribbean island of Curaçao, about 500 miles from St. Martin. Stuyvesant took several ships and hundreds of men with him on his expedition.

At first everything went well. His men splashed ashore without meeting any resistance, but it soon became apparent that the reports Stuyvesant had received were wrong. The Spanish had reinforced the fort with many soldiers. They began firing at the Dutch invaders.

For Stuyvesant, the unexpected resistance may have seemed like a good opportunity. His employer, the Dutch West India

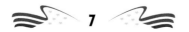

Company, already knew that he was an able administrator. Now he could show the company how brave he was in battle.

He ordered his men to protect themselves. As bullets and cannonballs whistled past them, they dug into the soft earth and erected a high wall of dirt. The troops took shelter behind the wall while Stuyvesant decided what to do next.

Soon he was ready. He grabbed a Dutch flag and clambered to the top of the wall. He hoped that when his troops saw the flag, it would raise their morale, helping them overcome their fear and encouraging them to follow him as he charged the fort.

He never got the chance to see if it would work. A cannonball shattered his right leg below the knee. He writhed on the ground in agony.

His men hauled him back behind the wall. In spite of his pain, he ordered them to continue the assault without him. Deprived of his leadership, they refused.

Stuyvesant's leg was so badly damaged that it would have to be amputated, or cut off. Amputation was a gruesome procedure.

"Typically, the patient, fully awake, was placed in a chair with two men holding him down," writes historian Russell Shorto. "The doctor would use his hands to 'pluck up the skin and muscles' of the limb in question, then, as one wrote, 'we cut the flesh with a razor or incising knife . . . to the bone, the said bone must be diligently rubbed and scraped with the back of the sayd knife, which back must be made purposely for that effect, to the end the periost [a layer of tissue with lots of nerve endings] which covereth the bone, may be lesse painfull in cutting of the bone. . . . This being done, you must saw the bone with sharpe saw."[1]

The agony of the knife slicing through muscles and the saw cutting through bone was awful. Then, to keep the patient from bleeding to death, exposed blood vessels had to be cauterized, or sealed by putting hot irons or boiling oil on them.

Anesthesia would not be discovered for another two centuries; before then, patients felt every slice and burn. Many patients got as drunk as possible in an effort to numb their nerves.

The procedure was also very dangerous. Many if not most people who lost limbs died anyway. A prominent English surgeon

of that time period wrote: "Let first your patient be well informed of the imminent danger of death by the use thereof; prescribe him no certainty of life, and let the work be done with his own free will and request, and not otherwise. Let him prepare his soul as a ready sacrifice to the Lord by earnest prayers . . . and forget thou not also thy dutie in that kinde, to crave mercie and help from the Almightie and that heartily."[2]

Stuyvesant undoubtedly followed the surgeon's advice and prayed a great deal. It helped that he was tough and young. He managed to survive the operation. For the following four weeks, he encouraged his dispirited troops to renew the attack on the fort. They refused every time. Finally he gave up. He and his men left St. Martin and sailed back to Curaçao. He wrote an apologetic (and understated) letter to his employers, telling them that the attack "did not succeed as well as I had hoped, no small impediment having been the loss of my right leg, it being removed by a rough ball."[3]

It became evident that his leg was not going to heal in the hot, humid Caribbean climate. His wound was likely to become infected in that atmosphere—and if it did, it could kill him.

Writing more than a century later, a surgeon named John Knyveton wrote, "It is almost always fatal to amputate a limb or digit in these Isles [in the Caribbean Sea], they always mortify [become infected] most furiously and the patient's condition being already lowered by the enervating air, soon sinks to rally no more."[4]

Stuyvesant's only hope was to go home to The Netherlands, where the climate was better and he would receive excellent medical care. To get there, he endured even more pain. The trip took months, and his ship was tossed about by storms. The agony of banging his bad leg against bulkheads and other obstacles must have been indescribable.

When he finally got home, he was fitted with a permanent wooden leg. Silver bands encircled it. Eventually, Peter Stuyvesant would be known as Pegleg Pete.

While he was recuperating, he stayed with his sister Anna and her husband, Samuel Bayard. Samuel's sister, Judith, also lived

with them. As she nursed Peter back to health, the two of them fell in love. Within a year they were married. They would have two children and a long life together.

Meanwhile, far across the ocean, a handful of Dutch settlers were clinging to a tiny colony in modern-day New York State. This colony had been established in 1624 by the Dutch West India Company. They had named it New Netherland, and its main settlement was the village of New Amsterdam on the southern tip of Manhattan Island. The current governor wasn't doing a very good job. He had provoked the local Indians into a bloody, destructive war. The conflict threatened the colony's very existence. Some of the most important men there had written a desperate letter to the company's directors, asking for a new governor.

By mid-spring in 1645, Stuyvesant's leg had healed. He reported to the Dutch West India Company's head office in Amsterdam, the capital of The Netherlands. He wanted the company's directors to know that he was ready to go back to work. His timing was perfect. The letter from New Netherland had arrived shortly before he did.

The company agreed they should replace the governor. Any serious problems in the colony hampered their ability to make a profit. They had just begun looking for a replacement, someone who was honest, brave, loyal to the company, and experienced in colonial affairs. Peter Stuyvesant had all these qualities and more.

The directors quickly appointed him as the new governor. Under his leadership, the colony would not just survive, it would thrive and grow in importance. Long after Stuyvesant's death, it would become one of the most important cities in the world: New York City, New York.

The Dutch West India Company

The Dutch West India Company tall ship Eendracht *(Unity)*

Christopher Columbus landed in the Americas in 1492. Five years later, Vasco da Gama began a voyage that established a sea route to Asia. European governments wanted to take advantage of the new opportunities for power and profit, but they didn't have enough money to do it themselves.

They quickly hit on a solution. They would grant charters to private companies. These companies acted almost as governments. They could fight battles, pass laws, and administer justice in the territories they controlled. In return, they gave their respective governments a small share of the profits and kept the rest for themselves and their shareholders.

The Dutch were among the leaders in this effort. A group of Dutch businessmen formed the East India Company in 1602. It made a great deal of money. India and other Asian countries had spices and other consumer goods that Europeans eagerly wanted—and for which they were willing to pay high prices.

The Dutch government followed the success of the East India Company by chartering the West India Company in 1621. It had the right to control trade in the Western Hemisphere—primarily the Caribbean, North America, and South America. The company established colonies in Brazil and on a number of Caribbean islands in addition to New Netherland. It even established a few stations on the west coast of Africa to take advantage of the developing slave trade.

After some successes, the company encountered hard times. One of its main sources of income was capturing Spanish merchant ships and selling their cargoes. That source ended when The Netherlands and Spain made peace in 1648. Another major setback came when the Portuguese drove the company out of Brazil a few years later. The French also captured some of the colonies the company had established in the Caribbean.

As a result of these reverses, the Dutch West India Company was reorganized in 1674 and resumed operations on a smaller scale. It went out of business for good more that a century later, in 1791.

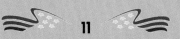

For Your Information

A metal plate on the outer wall of St. Mark's Church in New York City marks the tomb of Peter Stuyvesant. It states that Stuyvesant was born in 1572 and died at the age of eighty, but most historians agree this is a mistake. He was twenty years younger when he died.

CHAPTER
2

The Long Way to New York

It's not certain when Peter Stuyvesant was born. A stone tablet placed at his burial site correctly identifies the date of his death as February 1672, and includes the information that he was "aged 80 years." That would put the date of his birth sometime around 1592.

However, the tablet was not installed until nearly 100 years after his death. Most historians believe that the statement about his age is incorrect. They believe that it is much more likely that he was born between 1610 and 1612. One reason is an affidavit—a type of legal document—that Stuyvesant signed early in 1646. In this affidavit, Stuyvesant identifies himself as the "former Director of Curaçao in the service of the West India Company, about thirty-five years of age."[1] He was very careful about legal matters. It is highly doubtful that he would have signed something that contained any obvious errors—such as his age.

This much later birth date is consistent with several established facts. His father, a Calvinist minister named Balthazar Johannes Stuyvesant, began his college studies in 1605. It would have been very rare in that era for a man to start college at an age when he already had a teenage son. Another is that Peter's only

known sibling—his sister Anna—was born in 1613. A gap of twenty-one years between siblings is unusual. Finally, his father began his service at a new church with a note that "July 19, 1622, on Friday, am I, Balthazar Stuyvesant, with my wife and children come to live at Berlicum."[2] A man of thirty (Peter's age if he had been born in 1592) would hardly be described as a "child."

It seems certain that Peter Stuyvesant was born in the town of Scherpenzeel in the province of Friesland—one of the northernmost provinces of The Netherlands. He spent the first twelve or so years of his life there until his father's transfer to nearby Berlicum. Very little is known of how he was raised, except that as a minister's son he would have had a very strict upbringing.

The Netherlands always had a strong connection with the sea. Friesland would have been no exception. It lies on the shores of the Zuider Zee, a shallow inlet of the North Sea. As biographers Henry Kessler and Eugene Rachlis point out, "To a schoolboy in Friesland, lessons would have had to be a dry interlude between the exciting news of the war with Spain and the first-hand delight of watching the ships on the Zuider Zee going back and forth between Amsterdam and lands of adventure."[3]

Russell Shorto makes the same point. "Growing up, his literal horizon had been as low as they come; to a youth shaped by God and flat land, these vessels, jutting a hundred feet into the air, taller than anything he had seen, natural or man-made, great cathedrals of wood with spires promising real-world deliverance, must have made an impression."[4]

This impression may have been in the back of Stuyvesant's mind when he entered the University of Franeker, probably in 1628. In that era, many men were expected to take on the same occupations as their fathers. This expectation was especially high among the sons of ministers. Accordingly, it is likely that from an early age Peter and his parents planned for him to get a university education, which was necessary to become a minister. There was also no doubt that he would attend the University of Franeker. His father had graduated from the same school.

It didn't take long for these plans to fall apart. Stuyvesant lasted perhaps two years at the university. His name is still on

view in the school's records. Next to it is an image of the gallows—which indicates he was dismissed from the school for something disgraceful. It is not certain what it was. According to a widely circulated story, he had a love affair with his landlord's daughter. When the affair came to light, Peter was expelled.

No matter what the nature of his "crime," it was the last time that Peter Stuyvesant would knowingly act in a disgraceful manner. From that moment on, he presented himself as a model of moral behavior.

After college, he worked for the Dutch West India Company. His first job was probably as a clerk in the company's main office in Amsterdam, since everyone in the company started that way. Clerks learned how the company operated—and company officials learned how their employees operated. Officials found young Peter Stuyvesant to be a top-notch employee.

Within a few years the company sent Stuyvesant to Fernando de Noronha, a tiny island 200 miles off the coast of Brazil. In 1635 he was transferred to what is now called Recife on the Brazilian mainland. He must have done well there.

In 1638 he was appointed chief commercial officer for the island of Curaçao. The Dutch had taken the island from the Spanish four years earlier. Stuyvesant's main job was checking on captured ships and making sure that everything on board was delivered to Amsterdam. It was an important job for a man still in his twenties. It was also profitable. He received a substantial percentage of the value of those cargoes. On that basis, he ran up a heavy debt buying new clothes. He felt that he had to look like a successful businessman.

Stuyvesant continued to impress his superiors. Within four years he was named governor of Curaçao and the neighboring islands of Aruba and Bonaire. In addition to his other duties, he spent a lot of time planning how to capture St. Martin. The island had many valuable salt beds and tobacco plantations. Stuyvesant was convinced that regaining the island would lead to even higher promotions in the company.

Although he had never been in battle before, he was confident that he could capture the island without much trouble. Even after

New Amsterdam began as a cluster of modest buildings on the southern tip of Manhattan Island. It resembled its namesake city—the capital of The Netherlands—with its busy harbor, docks, and even a few windmills.

he was wounded, he stayed on the island for nearly a month. When his men refused to fight, he finally left. He bitterly said, it is "difficult to catch hares with unwilling dogs."[5]

The Dutch West India Company recognized that Stuyvesant, unlike his men, was very willing to do what they wanted. A year after the company had named him governor of New Netherland, the Dutch States-General—the country's ruling body—confirmed the appointment. Stuyvesant and his wife sailed for the New World in December 1646. He took a long detour that included a visit to Curaçao, then sailed into the harbor of New Amsterdam on May 11, 1647. He was about to take on the job that would make him famous.

The Netherlands and the Sea

By the time Peter Stuyvesant was born, Dutch ships were traveling to many parts of the world. They returned with expensive cargoes and fascinating tales of faraway lands. As he was growing up, Peter was enthralled.

He and his contemporaries had another reason for their interest in the sea. The North Sea, which forms the western border of the country, was a constant threat to their very existence. The Netherlands is very flat, and its highest point is only about 1,000 feet above sea level. In fact, the word *nether* means "below." More than one-fourth of the country is below sea level. About 60 percent of the country's inhabitants live in this region, much of which surrounded the Zuider Zee (ZY-dur ZEE, "southern sea" in Dutch). Another third of the country's surface area is no more than three feet above sea level. As a result, flooding remains a constant threat.

Delta Works in The Netherlands

When people began settling the region, they built dikes and similar structures in an effort to hold back the sea. They also built the country's picturesque windmills, many of which were used to pump floodwaters back into the sea. Today, electric pumps handle this important task.

Most of the time the Dutch have been successful in protecting themselves, but some especially strong storms have overcome their efforts. In 1287, more than 50,000 people drowned in the Zuider Zee when a seawall collapsed and the North Sea rushed inland. Another storm in 1953 killed nearly 2,000 people. That disaster launched a major program to prevent against future disasters. The result is collectively known as the North Sea Protective Works. It has been rated as one of the Seven Wonders of the Modern World by the American Society of Civil Engineers.

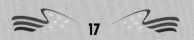

English explorer Henry Hudson entered New York Harbor in 1609 and sailed up the Hudson River in hopes of discovering a passage to Asia. He made another voyage the following year and discovered Hudson Bay. His crew mutinied and set him, his son, and a few other men adrift in a small boat. That was the last that anyone ever saw them.

CHAPTER
3

The Rise of New Amsterdam

In a roundabout way, Peter Stuyvesant owed his new job to the European craving for spices. These spices had to be imported from India and other Asian lands that were thousands of miles from Europe. Transporting them required a long and difficult journey, which made them very expensive. Europeans wanted to find a shorter, cheaper route.

When Christopher Columbus set out on his famous voyage in 1492, he was looking for that shorter route to the East. He didn't find it, but instead discovered the American continent, which lay between Europe and Asia. Many people believed the continent wasn't much of an obstacle. They were convinced that it contained a passage that would lead to the spice-growing countries.

In 1609, English explorer Henry Hudson was trying to locate this passage. His employer was the Dutch East India Company. He sailed into what today is known as New York Harbor, thinking he had found the way through the continent.

His excitement didn't last. He had discovered what would eventually be named the Hudson River, which is only about 300 miles long. When he realized his mistake, he sailed back to Europe. He believed that he had failed.

Although he had failed to find the passage, in another way, he had succeeded. Hats made of beaver fur were in great demand

in Europe. So many beavers had been killed in Europe to supply the hat making trade that they were almost extinct there. Hudson mentioned that many beavers lived in the region he had explored.

French traders in modern-day Canada were already sending back thousands of beaver pelts. Not unreasonably, they didn't want to share this bounty with the Dutch. Now, after Hudson's observation, the Dutch could establish their own beaver trade. They quickly claimed the region and called it New Netherland.

In 1621, the West India Company was formed to operate the new colony. Its purpose was to make as much money as possible for its investors. The first settlers arrived in 1624. Most went to Fort Orange, today's Albany, the best place to receive furs from the Indians. A few families settled on Governors Island in New York Harbor. The harbor was deep and sheltered, making it an ideal site for ships to tie up and take on cargoes of furs. The following year the families moved to the southern tip of Manhattan, built a fort, and founded the village of New Amsterdam.

The settlement soon surpassed Fort Orange in importance. In 1626, the newly appointed governor of New Netherland, Peter Minuit (min-WEE), "bought" the island from the Indians. Even more people settled there. Minuit built a small fort and improved the quality of the housing for the inhabitants. He also widened a path that led northward into the forested interior, and over to the fish-rich inlets on the island's eastern side. The Dutch called it *breede weg*, or "wide way." The street is the modern-day home of the American theater industry, famous in its English translation as Broadway.

But such fame was still far off. The community didn't immediately thrive. Many of the new arrivals did not want to work hard. The colony's secretary said, "I cannot wonder at the lazy unconcern of many persons, both farmers and others, who are willing enough to draw their rations and pay in return for doing almost nothing."[1]

As a result, the colony did not produce much profit for the West India Company. This poor showing contrasted sharply with the company's success in the Caribbean. The directors wanted New Netherland to pull its own weight. When they heard that

As the second director-general, or governor, of New Netherland, Peter Minuit (center) is best known for his trades with the Lenni Lenape, or Delaware, tribe. He traded trinkets worth approximately $24 for Manhattan Island.

Minuit was cheating the company and using his position to make money for himself, the directors fired him in 1631.

His replacement, Wouter van Twiller, didn't do any better. He proved to be incompetent in virtually every area of administration.

On one occasion, he fired off a cannon. Sparks ignited the roof of a nearby house and the structure burned to the ground. On the other hand, he was very skilled at buying property. He eventually became a wealthy man.

Willem Kieft succeeded van Twiller in 1637. Two years later, he tried to impose a tax on the local Indians. Not surprisingly, the Indians refused to pay it. The settlers were outraged at Kieft's action. They depended on the good will of the Indians to keep

Willem Kieft (in red) plots with Dutch colleagues against the Indians. Kieft's War, which lasted from 1643 to 1645, would claim the lives of at least 1,000 Indians.

them provided with furs. Whatever else van Twiller's faults may have been, he had stayed on good terms with the Indians.

Over the next few years, the Indians became increasingly aggressive. On a few occasions, they murdered individual settlers in outlying areas. Kieft demanded that their chiefs turn over the killers to him. His demands were refused. Kieft seethed with resentment at this defiance of his authority. He wanted revenge. In 1643, against the advice of the colony's prominent citizens, Kieft and dozens of soldiers attacked an Indian village while its residents were sleeping.

Their actions were brutal. "Infants were torn from their mothers' breasts, and hacked to pieces in the presence of the parents, and the pieces thrown into the fire and the water," wrote David De Vries, a Dutch trader. "Some came to our people in the country with their hands, some with their legs cut off, and some holding their entrails [stomach and intestines] in their arms."[2]

At least 100 Indians died in the massacre. Other Indians retaliated. It became dangerous for settlers to live anywhere except in New Amsterdam itself. Over the next two years, hundreds died on both sides. Finally, the combatants—thoroughly tired and depressed from the constant warfare—agreed not to fight anymore.

For Kieft, the reprieve came too late. With complaints from settlers and the almost complete standstill in the fur trade, Kieft was dismissed. He would not leave the island empty-handed. According to one estimate, he had amassed a fortune of 400,000 guilders[3]—nearly 7,000 times the amount of money that had been given to the Indians for the "purchase" of Manhattan Island two decades earlier. (Ironically, Kieft would never make it home. When he did eventually leave the colony, his ship was lost at sea.)

The colonists had been so unhappy with Kieft, they gave Stuyvesant an exuberant reception when his ship dropped anchor in the harbor. The small fort fired its cannons until the gunpowder was exhausted. The townspeople swarmed down to the waterfront to see the new governor. As the small rowboat carrying him grew steadily closer, they began cheering loudly. When the boat landed, they applauded.

Two Dutch settlers take a casual stroll along a canal in New Amsterdam. The man on the porch and another man on the road behind them smoke long pipes, which were especially popular during that era.

Even Stuyvesant, who rarely smiled, must have felt gratified. There could have been no doubt in his mind that this was the high point in his career. He was confident that he could reshape New Netherland in his own image—honest, law-abiding, and profitable. He must have looked forward to making it the jewel in the crown of the Dutch West India Company.

"Buying" Manhattan Island

Dutch guilders were one of many types of money used in New Netherland

Many people believe that Peter Minuit purchased Manhattan Island from the local Indians for 60 guilders, or $24. There is no way to verify what actually happened, but it seems likely that at least part of the story is true. If so, it is one of the greatest land transactions—or swindles—in history. In 1990, historian Oliver Allen commented: "Manhattan real estate is estimated to be worth a total of $30 billion."[4]

Minuit was born sometime between 1580 and 1589. He probably began working for the Dutch West India Company in the early 1620s, and was appointed governor of New Netherland in 1625. He arrived in May the following year, and reportedly his "deal" with the Indians took place soon afterward. The only evidence for the transaction is a letter written by a Dutch official named Pieter Schaghen, which says that Minuit "purchased the Island Manhattes from the Indians for the value of 60 guilders; it is 11,000 morgens [about 23,000 acres] in size."[5] A guilder was a Dutch coin; the figure of $24 was determined around 200 years later as an estimate of the guilder's buying power at the time of Minuit's purchase.

The transaction would have consisted of trade goods, not cash. When Minuit bought Staten Island five years later, the payment included "Duffels [cloth], Kittles [kettles], Axes, Hoes, Wampum, Drilling Awls, Jews Harps, and diverse other small wares."[6] It is likely that he used similar goods to purchase Manhattan.

Even the word *purchase* is misleading. The Indians had no concept of buying and selling property. Rather, they believed they were simply allowing the Dutch the right to live on the land, alongside the Indians. Since the island was mostly wilderness and there weren't many people—either Dutch or Indians—there was plenty of room for both groups. The Manhattan Indians continued to live there until about 1680, when they moved across the East River to the modern-day Bronx.

By then Peter Minuit was long gone from New Netherland. He helped to establish the rival colony of New Sweden in 1638 near the site of modern-day Wilmington, Delaware. He died later that year when the ship he was aboard sank during a hurricane in the Caribbean.

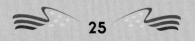

The Dutch colonists built a wall across Manhattan to guard against invasions. The wall was taken down several years later, but the path that ran along the wall remains as Wall Street. It is the center of the U.S. financial industry.

CHAPTER 4

Governor Stuyvesant

Once the expressions of welcome died down, Stuyvesant realized that he faced a difficult task. Many of the houses were little more than shanties. The town stank because people threw their garbage into the streets, hoping the pigs and other animals that roamed freely would eventually eat it. They also threw out their sewage. The fort that was supposed to protect hundreds of people was, he wrote, "more a mole-hill than a fortress, without gates, the walls and bastions trodden underfoot by men and cattle."[1]

His first changes were practical. Streets meandered through New Amsterdam. He wanted to straighten them and make them more uniform. He also wanted to keep them as free as possible of livestock and debris—in particular, human excrement. Because of the danger of fire, he banned wooden chimneys and ordered that the rest be cleaned.

Perhaps the colonists' most dangerous trait was the open contempt they felt toward Kieft, who had not yet returned to The Netherlands. Whatever his faults, Kieft had been the legally appointed leader of the colony. In Stuyvesant's eyes, Kieft deserved to be respected because of his former position.

Stuyvesant thought he knew just what to do to restore this respect. "I shall govern you as a father his children,"[2] he said.

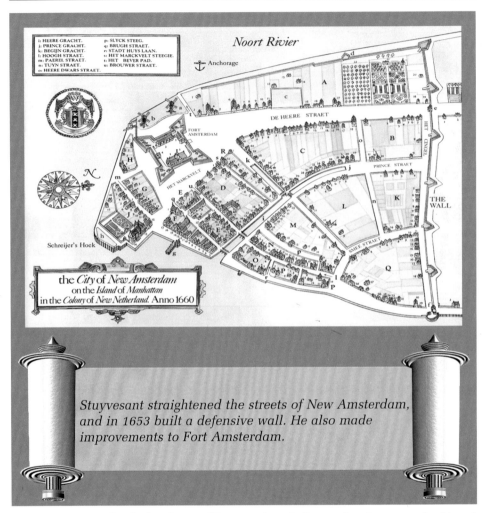

the *City* of *New Amsterdam*
on the *Island* of *Manhattan*
in the *Colony* of *New Netherland.* Anno 1660

Stuyvesant straightened the streets of New Amsterdam, and in 1653 built a defensive wall. He also made improvements to Fort Amsterdam.

The way in which he formally received the colonists symbolized this attitude. He greeted them sitting down while they remained standing. He wore his hat while they removed theirs. These actions reinforced his authority.

Like many fathers, he was convinced that he knew what was best for his "children." Like children, however, the colonists often disagreed with their "father." These inevitable disagreements were magnified because the "children" were very different from one another. Unlike other colonies in the New World, New Netherland had attracted a wide variety of people. While many were Dutch, people from other countries in Europe lived there as

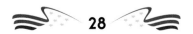

well. As Jesuit missionary Isaac Jogues noted, "On the island of Manhate and its environs, there may well be four or five hundred men of different sects or nations: the Director-General [Kieft] told me that there were men of eighteen different languages."[3] Governing people from so many cultures would be difficult.

It would be even more difficult because Stuyvesant was stubborn. He didn't like people who disagreed with him. As events would soon show, the people in New Netherland frequently disagreed with him—and they were just as stubborn as he.

The first major disagreement surfaced a few days after his arrival. Two drunken men got into a knife fight on Sunday afternoon.

No matter what their backgrounds were, nearly all the citizens of New Amsterdam loved to drink. The drinking usually began at breakfast, continued through the day, and didn't end until late at night. Even children were accustomed to consuming alcoholic beverages.

As a result of the knife fight, Stuyvesant forbade the sale of alcohol on Sundays. He explained: "We see and observe by experience the great disorders in which some of our inhabitants indulge, in drinking to excess, quarreling, fighting . . . even on the Lord's day of rest."[4] Other restrictions on drinking alcohol soon followed.

The people who had cheered so heartily just a few weeks before quickly changed their minds about their new governor. Straightening streets was one thing. Not letting them drink as much as they wanted was quite another. Stuyvesant's popularity plummeted even further when he announced that he would impose taxes to pay for the civic improvements.

Stuyvesant was no fool. He knew the people didn't like what he was doing. He decided to reach out to them—sort of. He announced the formation of a Board of Nine, which would serve as an advisory group of eighteen men. From those, Stuyvesant would pick the nine he wanted. However, he made it clear that he wouldn't take their advice if he didn't want to.

Animosity began to bubble to the surface. Two men, Joachim Kuyter and Cornelius Melyn, filed a lawsuit against Kieft. They argued that when the Indians had attacked during Kieft's administration, their property had been destroyed. The two men wanted compensation.

Stuyvesant had to support either the unpopular Kieft or the colonists. Choosing Kieft, he found the two men guilty of sedition, the encouragement of rebellion. In his mind, sedition was a very serious crime. To discourage another attack on the lawful authority of the governor, he ordered the two men to be hanged.

The Board of Nine protested the severity of the sentence. Stuyvesant listened to them. He decided not to execute the two men. Instead, he ordered them to leave the colony.

Kuyter and Melyn sailed back to The Netherlands and appealed their banishment to the Dutch government, which supported them. Melyn returned to New Amsterdam in 1649, receiving the same sort of exuberant welcome that had greeted Stuyvesant just two years earlier. His success encouraged another group of men, led by a prosperous landowner named Adriaen van der Donck, to send a petition to the Dutch government. It spelled out Stuyvesant's shortcomings. They too were successful.

The government issued a written order to Stuyvesant to set up a system of government similar to those of free cities in The Netherlands. He eventually did, though he appointed the men who held all the important offices. The document also contained an ominous phrase: "Petrus Stuyvesant, the present Director, shall be instructed to return home and report."[5] In other words, Stuyvesant was being recalled. There was a very good chance that once back in The Netherlands, he would never see New Amsterdam again.

Before Stuyvesant could comply with his order of recall, the colony faced a serious threat from the English. There was no chance the directors would fire him in the face of this crisis.

The English had already established substantial footholds in North America. Their first colony—Jamestown, Virginia— was more than 40 years old. They were especially active in New England. They had founded the Plymouth Colony in 1620, followed by several additional colonies nearby. By 1650, the English controlled much more territory in North

America than the Dutch. Their territory also contained many more people.

The boundaries between the two nations' territorial claims had never been firmly established. The Dutch and the English claimed a great deal of what is present-day Connecticut. Stuyvesant traveled to Connecticut to try to agree on the borders. He didn't have much leverage. He believed that the English in the region outnumbered him fifty to one. While the actual figure was much lower—probably about fifteen to one—it was still a considerable imbalance. Nevertheless, he negotiated an agreement called the Treaty of Hartford. It helped the two sides get along.

Two years later, a war between The Netherlands and England broke out in Europe. English settlers took advantage of the situation to begin moving closer to New Amsterdam. Many settled on the eastern side of Long Island, only a few miles from Dutch colonists clustered on the western tip. A fleet of ships full of English soldiers sailed to Boston Harbor. An invasion seemed imminent.

Stuyvesant wanted to improve New Amsterdam's defenses. Under his orders, the citizens constructed a fortified wall along the northern edge of the settlement in 1653. A path ran next to the wall. The effort proved to be unnecessary. Early the following year, the English and Dutch governments reached an agreement that ended what would be known as the First Anglo-Dutch War.

The path, however, proved to be much more permanent. Soon it was widened. Because it was next to the fortified wall, it was called Wall Street. Today, Wall Street is the center of the U.S. financial industry. News commentators often refer to Wall Street as a symbol of how the country's economy is doing. It was just one of many names in New York originally given by the Dutch that have endured to the present age.

Conflict soon arose from another direction. Nine years before Stuyvesant's arrival, the vengeful Peter Minuit—now employed by the Swedish government—had helped establish a rival colony called New Sweden. It lay within 100 miles of New Amsterdam on land along the Delaware River. The colony wasn't very large, never numbering more than 300 people. It didn't present much

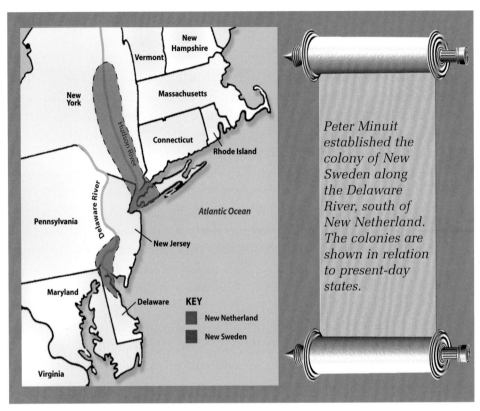

Peter Minuit established the colony of New Sweden along the Delaware River, south of New Netherland. The colonies are shown in relation to present-day states.

of a threat, but the Dutch believed this land was theirs, and Stuyvesant resented the colony's existence.

In 1651, Stuyvesant had ordered a fort to be built on the Delaware River close to similar fortifications in New Sweden. Three years later, an aggressive new governor named Johan Rising arrived in New Sweden. He ordered Stuyvesant's fort to surrender. Stuyvesant was outraged.

After the First Anglo-Dutch War, England no longer posed an immediate threat to New Amsterdam. Stuyvesant took hundreds of men from his colony and besieged New Sweden. The campaign may have reminded him of the battle in the Caribbean in which he had lost his leg. This time the outcome was far more favorable. Rising surrendered without a fight. New Sweden ceased to exist. Its territory became part of New Netherland.

Stuyvesant had been successful in maintaining peace with Indians. However, while he was gone on this expedition, a settler

shot an Indian who was stealing peaches from his orchard. What followed became known as the Peach War.

Knowing that Stuyvesant had left New Amsterdam virtually undefended, hundreds of Indians landed from their canoes and swarmed through the town. They could have massacred nearly everyone. While they decided not to, shooting eventually broke out. Dozens of people on both sides lost their lives. When he heard the news, Stuyvesant rushed back and quickly negotiated an end to the hostilities. Some of the colonists urged him to keep fighting to seek revenge. He replied, "The recent war is to be attributed to the rashness of a few hotheaded individuals. It becomes us to reform ourselves, to abstain from all wrong, and to guard against a recurrence of the late unhappy affair."[6]

It was the final time that Indians would threaten New Amsterdam. The town entered a period of peace and stability. According to some estimates, the population increased three- or fourfold, to about 8,000, in less than a decade. Ships delivering cargoes to the inhabitants reflected that prosperity. Russell Shorto notes: "The new products appearing in New Amsterdam's shops speak of a more refined life for its inhabitants—medicine, measuring equipment, damask, fine writing paper, oranges and lemons, parakeets and parrots, saffron, sassafras, and sarsaparilla."[7]

Stuyvesant's strict Calvinist upbringing may have helped the colony in some ways, but it also had a dark side. While there was supposedly freedom of religion in the colony, he did not extend it to everyone.

In 1654, the Portuguese captured Pernambuco, a Dutch colony in Brazil, and expelled about twenty-three Jews who had been living there. They arrived in New Amsterdam without any money. Stuyvesant wanted to get rid of them, using their lack of money as a justification. The company directors (influenced at least in part by its Jewish stockholders) decided that they could stay—as long as they didn't become a "burden."

By the time they reached that decision in the spring of 1655, another group of Jews had sailed to the colony from The Netherlands. Their arrival spurred the first anti-Semitic document in the New World. A minister named Jacob Megapolensis wrote that they would cause "a great deal of complaint and murmuring. These people have no other God than the Mammon of unrighteousness, and no other aim than to get possession of Christian property, and to overcome all other merchants by drawing all trade toward themselves. . . . These godless rascals . . . are of no benefit to the country, but look at everything for their own profit."[8] He sided with Stuyvesant in urging them to be deported.

Again the company refused the request. Stuyvesant used his power to make their lives miserable. He placed restrictions on their movements, including their ability to buy property and to sell merchandise. They couldn't even hire servants. Fed up with these conditions, most of them left the colony.

Stuyvesant also discriminated against the Quakers. In 1657, two Quaker women managed to come ashore and began preaching. He immediately arrested them, tied their hands behind their backs, and had them returned to the ship from which they had landed. In response, citizens of Flushing, a town on Long Island, sent Stuyvesant a letter protesting his anti-Quaker actions. Eventually the document, called the Flushing Remonstrance, reached the West India Company, which sided with the colonists. The company insisted that Stuyvesant allow religious freedom.

But there was nothing Stuyvesant could do to end the steady pressure from New England. The uneasy situation continued into the early 1660s. Stuyvesant continually sent letters to the company directors, asking for more money and more men to defend New Netherland. The directors always turned him down. For a number of reasons, the company wasn't doing well financially. They couldn't afford to help Stuyvesant.

While Stuyvesant was writing his letters, events in England were about to have a profound impact on the fate of New Netherland—and on its governor.

Dutch Place-Names in New York

Bouwerij is the Dutch word for farm, and Stuyvesant's farm was one of the largest. After his death, it became the Bowery, a fashionable New York neighborhood. By the end of the nineteenth century, however, the neighborhood had become disreputable. After another hundred years, the Bowery began returning to its former elegance.

Greenwich Village, another neighborhood in Manhattan, was originally known to the Indians as *Sapokanikan* ("tobacco field"). The Dutch renamed it *Noortwyck* (North District). When a settler from the village of *Greenwyck* (Pine District) on Long Island relocated to Noortwyck, he brought that name with him.

In 1658, Stuyvesant founded the town of Nieuw (New) Haarlem several miles north of New Amsterdam for "lovers of agriculture." He gave the settlers there farmland and meadowland. Now it is a neighborhood called Harlem.

The Bronx is named for Jonas Bronck, who established a farm north of Manhattan in 1641. Today the Bronx is one of five boroughs that make up New York City.

The city of Yonkers is next to the Bronx. Its first settler was Adriaen van der Donck—the lawyer who had petitioned the Dutch government about Stuyvesant's shortcomings. His nickname was the Young Gentleman, or *Jonkheer* (YON-kayr). The city's name comes from his nickname.

The Brooklyn Bridge connects Brooklyn and Manhattan

Some settlers built homes on the southwestern end of Long Island. They named their village *Breuckelen*, after a town in The Netherlands. Known today as Brooklyn, it is the largest of New York City's five boroughs. A creek separated Brooklyn from a small island with many rabbits, which the Dutch named *Conyne Eylandt* (Rabbit Island). Many modern-day New Yorkers enjoy the beach and boardwalk at Coney Island.

Flatbush is a neighborhood in Brooklyn. Established in 1651, its name comes from *Vladbos*, or "wooded land." Flushing is a neighborhood in the borough of Queens. Founded in 1645, its original name was *Vlissingen*, which means "salt meadow."

Explorer Henry Hudson named an island in New York Harbor *Staaten Eylandt* in 1609 after the *Staaten-Generaal*, the Dutch parliament. Today we know it as Staten Island, the southernmost of the five New York City boroughs.

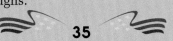

Peter Stuyvesant was very rigid in his beliefs. When anyone disagreed with him, he would become very angry. Waving his cane was one way that he showed his anger.

CHAPTER
5

New York, New York

In 1642, a series of civil wars began in England. Forces loyal to King Charles I were eventually defeated. The king was captured and beheaded. Led by Oliver Cromwell, England became a republic rather than a monarchy—but Cromwell's leadership was shaky. He and his followers were more concerned with keeping power than in handling foreign affairs, though they did fight the brief war with the Dutch in 1652. Cromwell died six years later. The monarchy was restored in 1660 when Charles II, the son of the deposed king, became the country's ruler.

Charles, who still considered the Dutch to be his rivals, began the Second Anglo-Dutch War. One obvious target was the thriving colony of New Netherland. In 1664, the king granted his younger brother James, the Duke of York, the right to take over large portions of the New World. The grant included New Netherland. Using his own money, James raised an army of hundreds of men and four ships. Colonel Richard Nicholls was made commander of the force.

James's preparations were no secret. Stuyvesant knew that Nicholls and his men were coming. There was very little he could do except wait for their arrival.

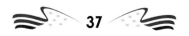

On August 26, the English fleet dropped anchor near the southern tip of Manhattan. Nicholls's troops poured ashore on Long Island, directly across from New Amsterdam. But Nicholls didn't want a fight. Instead, he sent a letter with surrender terms to Stuyvesant. These terms were very lenient. None of the town's inhabitants would have to give up their homes or businesses. He also made it clear that he didn't intend to do anything that would change their way of life.

Stuyvesant remained defiant. He tore up the letter without telling anyone about its contents. Then he climbed to the top of his fort, pointed a cannon toward the English fleet, and prepared to light it.

That was as far as he got. Nicholls's surrender terms had leaked out. Apparently Stuyvesant was the only man in New Amsterdam who didn't want to accept them. A group of prominent citizens talked him out of fighting a hopeless battle. They knew the damage and deaths that would result if the English seamen opened fire. They even presented him with a document signed by nearly 100 of the town's leading citizens.

"On all sides we are encompassed and hemmed in by our enemies," it read. "[The fort] cannot save the smallest portion of our entire city, our property and (what is dearer to us) our wives and children, from total ruin."[1]

If Stuyvesant glanced at the signatures, he would have recognized them all, especially the second name on the list: Balthazar, his older son. Stuyvesant complied with their wishes. He raised a white flag over the fort, though he wasn't happy about it.

"I had rather be carried to my grave,"[2] he said.

The English quickly renamed the settlement New York in honor of James, the Duke of York. Nearly all the settlers chose to remain, including Peter Stuyvesant. Since arriving in the New World in the early 1630s, he had been back to The Netherlands only once—when he was recuperating from the loss of his leg. Except for short trips away from the colony on official business, he had lived continuously in New Netherland ever since his arrival there. Both his sons had been born there.

Peter Stuyvesant leads his soldiers out of New Amsterdam to surrender to the English in 1664. He had wanted to fight the invaders, but coolheaded citizens handed him a petition urging him to give up and avoid bloodshed. His own son was one of the signers.

He did have one obligation after Nicholls took over as governor. He had to go to The Netherlands to explain his decision to surrender. He probably assumed that it would take a short time. He was mistaken.

The Dutch government wanted a scapegoat—someone to blame—for losing New Netherland. The company didn't want to admit that the loss was their own fault. After all, they could have given Stuyvesant the support he had asked for. Placing all the responsibility on him, they accused Stuyvesant of being a liar and a coward. They had plenty of ammunition. Stuyvesant had

made numerous enemies during his term as governor, and these enemies were happy to testify against him.

Naturally Stuyvesant was angry. He didn't like having his reputation called into question. He spent more than three years rebutting the charges. Finally, in the spring of 1668, he was able to return to New York. No longer interested in politics, he lived quietly on his farm until his death in February 1672.

There was a flurry of excitement a year and a half later. The Dutch and the French declared war on each other. The English supported the French and took advantage of the conflict to attack Dutch shipping. In retaliation, the Dutch sent a large fleet and hundreds of soldiers to retake New Netherland. New York became New Orange in honor of William of Orange, an important Dutch official. When the countries called for peace in 1674, the Dutch once again agreed to give up New Netherland. The last official statement that a Dutch governor of New Netherland would ever write was dated November 10, 1674. The capital once again became New York.

The Dutch control in New York had finally ended, but its influence would continue. And no one is more closely connected with this influence than Peter Stuyvesant.

Historian Edward Robb Ellis points out numerous firsts that occurred during the Stuyvesant era: the first pier on the East River, the first Latin school, the first law to regulate speed, the first hospital, the first post office, the first unemployment relief act, the first city directory, the first public market, and many others.[3] There was yet another first during Stuyvesant's time. As Ellis notes, "In 1657 Jacques Cortelyou became the first commuter by traveling daily between his Long Island home and Manhattan."[4] Thousands of men and women follow the trail that Cortelyou blazed by pouring into Manhattan from their suburban homes every weekday.

Nevertheless, because Dutch control of New Netherland was so short-lived, the memory of Stuyvesant's tenure as governor—positive and negative—probably would have faded into the mists of time. However, in 1809, Washington Irving wrote *A History of New York*, under the pen name Diedrich Knickerbocker.

Stuyvesant was the hero of the book, which became very popular. The book insured that Stuyvesant's legacy would endure.

Irving's use of "Knickerbocker" as his pen name would also leave a legacy. Today a resident of New York who can trace his or her family back to the original Dutch settlers is referred to as a Knickerbocker. The name has also become identified with New York sports teams. The New York Knicks compete with other teams in the National Basketball Association.

Stuyvesant's name lives on in New York City in Stuyvesant High School. Not surprisingly, its football team is known as the Peglegs. On a more serious level, the high school was one of the first three Specialized High Schools of New York City (in 2007, there were nine), which serve the area's outstanding students. Admittance is by examination only.

The school is a fitting testament to Peter Stuyvesant. Education was one of his top priorities. When he arrived, there was no one to teach school. "We need a pious and diligent schoolmaster," he said. "Our young people have gone backward, even to grow wild. . . . A good schoolmaster is not less needed here than a good preacher."[5]

There is ample evidence that Stuyvesant High School has provided its share of "good schoolmasters." At least four of its graduates have gone on to win Nobel Prizes. Pegleg Pete would be proud of their accomplishments.

Washington Irving

U.S. author Washington Irving (1783–1859)

Washington Irving was born in New York City in 1783, the year the peace treaty ending the Revolutionary War was signed. He was named for George Washington. Just as George Washington is known as the "father of his country," Irving is frequently referred to as the "father of American literature." He was the first American to make a living solely by writing.

Growing up, he was very fond of books and read a great deal. As a young man he worked as a lawyer and contributed to newspapers. After the success of *A History of New York* in 1809, he wrote a number of short stories over the following decade. The most famous are "Rip Van Winkle" (about a man who takes a nap one afternoon and wakes up twenty years later) and "The Headless Horseman." These short stories were published as *The Sketch Book of Geoffrey Crayon* in 1820. It established his reputation, especially in Europe where he was regarded as the first important American writer.

He traveled extensively in Europe, meeting such famous writers as Mary Shelley (the author of *Frankenstein*), Sir Walter Scott, and Charles Dickens. Soon after returning in 1832, he toured in the western United States—at that time a considerable adventure—and wrote more books about his experiences. These books added to his wealth and fame. He purchased a large home on the Hudson River in New York.

Irving served as the U.S. ambassador to Spain from 1842 to 1845. He spent most of the rest of his life writing a biography of George Washington and working with what later became the New York Public Library. He died in 1859. His home, which he named Sunnyside, remains a popular tourist destination.

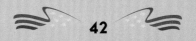

Chapter Notes

Chapter 1
The Man with the Wooden Leg
1. Russell Shorto, *The Island at the Center of the World* (New York: Doubleday, 2004), p. 147.
2. Ibid.
3. Henry H. Kessler and Eugene Rachlis, *Peter Stuyvesant and His New York* (New York: Random House, 1959), p. 48.
4. Ibid.

Chapter 2
The Long Way to New York
1. Henry H. Kessler and Eugene Rachlis, *Peter Stuyvesant and His New York* (New York: Random House, 1959), p. 286.
2. Ibid.
3. Ibid., p. 38.
4. Russell Shorto, *The Island at the Center of the World* (New York: Doubleday, 2004), p. 148.
5. Kessler and Rachlis, p. 47.

Chapter 3
The Rise of New Amsterdam
1. Henry H. Kessler and Eugene Rachlis, *Peter Stuyvesant and His New York* (New York: Random House, 1959), p. 41.
2. Ibid., p. 57.
3. Edward Robb Ellis, *The Epic of New York City* (New York: Coward-McCann, 1966), p. 44.
4. Oliver Allen, *New York, New York* (New York: Atheneum, 1990), p. 15.
5. Russell Shorto, *The Island at the Center of the World* (New York: Doubleday, 2004), p. 55.
6. Ibid., p. 56.

Chapter 4
Governor Stuyvesant
1. Edwin G. Burrows and Mike Wallace, *Gotham: A History of New York City to 1898* (New York: Oxford University Press, 1989), p. 42.
2. Ibid., p. 43.
3. Henry H. Kessler and Eugene Rachlis, *Peter Stuyvesant and His New York* (New York: Random House, 1959), p. 7.
4. Oliver Allen, *New York, New York* (New York: Atheneum, 1990), p. 23.
5. Russell Shorto, *The Island at the Center of the World* (New York: Doubleday, 2004), p. 230.
6. Allen, pp. 28–29.
7. Shorto, p. 268.
8. Ted Morgan, *Wilderness at Dawn: The Settling of the North American Continent* (New York: Simon & Schuster, 1993), p. 160.

Chapter 5
New York, New York
1. Henry H. Kessler and Eugene Rachlis, *Peter Stuyvesant and His New York* (New York: Random House, 1959), pp. 267–268.
2. Edward Robb Ellis, *The Epic of New York City* (New York: Coward-McCann, 1966), p. 70.
3. Ibid., p. 45.
4. Ibid.
5. Kessler and Rachlis, p. 119.

Chronology

1610	Likely date of Peter Stuyvesant's birth in The Netherlands
1622	Moves with family to Berlicum
1628–29	Enrolls at University of Franeker
1630	Is forced to leave the University of Franeker, begins work with the Dutch West India Company
c. 1632	Is sent by Dutch West India Company to island of Fernando de Noronha
1635	Transfers to Recife, Brazil
1638	Is appointed chief commercial officer of Curaçao, Aruba, and Bonaire
1642	Is appointed governor of Curaçao
1644	Leg is amputated after battle on St. Martin
1645	Returns to The Netherlands; is appointed governor of New Netherland
1646	Marries Judith Bayard
1647	Arrives in New Amsterdam, New Netherland colony
1650	Negotiates Treaty of Hartford
1653	Incorporates New Amsterdam; builds wall on north side of settlement, bordering a path that will eventually become Wall Street
1655	Attacks New Sweden; negotiates end to Peach War
1656	Denies Jews the right to build a synagogue in New Amsterdam
1657	Arrests two Quaker women; Long Island citizens respond with open meetings and write the Flushing Remonstrance
1664	Surrenders New Netherland to the English
1665	Is summoned to Holland to explain his actions in surrendering New Netherland
1668	Returns to New York to farm the Bowery
1672	Dies in New York

Timeline in History

1558	Elizabeth I becomes Queen of England.
1565	Spanish explorer Pedro Menéndez de Avilés founds St. Augustine, Florida, the oldest city in the United States.
1588	English defeat the Spanish Armada.
1602	The Dutch East India Company is founded.
1603	Elizabeth dies and is succeeded by her nephew, James I.
1607	English found colony at Jamestown, Virginia.
1609	Henry Hudson sails up the Hudson River.
1610	Henry Hudson discovers Hudson Bay in Canada.
1614	Powhatan's daughter Pocahontas marries Virginia settler John Rolfe.
1619	First slaves from Africa arrive in Virginia colony.
1620	Pilgrims land at Plymouth, Massachusetts.
1621	The Dutch West India Company is established.
1625	New Amsterdam is founded.
1625	Charles I becomes King of England.
1626	Peter Minuit "buys" Manhattan Island from the Indians.
1630	Boston, Massachusetts, is founded.
1639	The first printing press in North America is established in Cambridge, Massachusetts.
1649	Charles I is executed.
1652	The First Anglo-Dutch War begins; it will end in 1654.
1653	Oliver Cromwell becomes Lord Protector of England and assumes dictatorial powers.
1660	Charles II becomes King of England.
1664	Second Anglo-Dutch War begins; it will last until 1667.
1666	Great Fire of London burns for four days and destroys more than 10,000 houses and other buildings.
1672	Dutch inventor Jan van der Heiden introduces the first flexible hose for fighting fires.
1673	Dutch recapture New York and rename it New Orange, but they depart just over a year later, ending the Third Anglo-Dutch War; the city's name reverts to New York.
1682	William Penn founds the city of Philadelphia, Pennsylvania.
1685	Charles II dies and his brother, the Duke of York, becomes King James II.
1706	Benjamin Franklin is born.
1729	Baltimore, Maryland, is founded.

Further Reading

For Young Adults

Banks, Joan. *Peter Stuyvesant: Dutch Military Leader*. Hempstead, Texas: Sagebrush, 1999.

Johnston, Lissa. *A Brief Political and Geographic History of North America*. Hockessin, Delaware: Mitchell Lane Publishers, 2008.

Krizner, L. J., and Lisa Sita. *Peter Stuyvesant: New Amsterdam and the Origins of New York*. New York: PowerPlus Books, 2002.

Maestro, Betsy. *The New Americans: Colonial Times, 1620–1689*. New York: Lothrop, Lee & Shepard Books, 1998.

Works Consulted

Allen, Oliver E. *New York, New York: A History of the World's Most Exhilarating and Challenging City*. New York: Atheneum, 1990.

Burrows, Edwin G., and Mike Wallace. *Gotham: A History of New York City to 1898*. New York: Oxford University Press, 1989.

Ellis, Edward Robb. *The Epic of New York City*. New York: Coward-McCann, 1966.

Kessler, Henry H., and Eugene Rachlis. *Peter Stuyvesant and His New York*. New York: Random House, 1959.

Morgan, Ted. *Wilderness at Dawn: The Settling of the North American Continent*. New York: Simon & Schuster, 1993.

Quinn, Arthur. *A New World: An Epic of Colonial America from the Founding of Jamestown to the Fall of Quebec*. New York: Berkley Books, 1994.

Shepherd, William R. *The Story of New Amsterdam*. Port Washington, New York: Kennikat Press, 1970.

Shorto, Russell. *The Island at the Center of the World*. New York: Doubleday, 2004.

On the Internet

Abbott, John S. C. *John Peter Stuyvesant, the Last Dutch Governor of New Amsterdam*. http://www.gutenberg.org/files/13811/13811-8.txt

Anderson, John D. "Washington Irving." http://pages.emerson.edu/faculty/J/John_Anderson/e_irving.htm

Beck, Sanderson. "English, French, and Dutch Colonies 1643–1664." http://san.beck.org/11-5-Colonies1643-64.html

New Netherland Institute: "Minuit, Peter." http://www.nnp.org/nni/Publications/Dutch-American/minuit.html

Peck, Claude J. "September Song." April 3, 2000. http://www.chilit.org/PECK1.HTM

Roosevelt, Theodore. "Stuyvesant and the End of Dutch Rule, 1647–1664." 1906. http://www.bartleby.com/171/3.html

Washington Irving http://classicreader.com/author.php/aut.60/

Glossary

affidavit (ah-fuh-DAY-vit)
A legal document swearing
something is true.

bulkheads (BULK-heds)
Partitions that divide the hull
of a ship into several smaller
compartments.

Calvinist (KAL-vih-nist)
A follower of the Protestant
religion founded by John Calvin,
which stresses one God, the
sinfulness of mankind, and
the belief that life's events are
determined before they are lived.

**compensation
(kom-pen-SAY-shun)**
Payment that makes up for
losses and suffering endured as a
result of another's wrongdoing.

damask (duh-MASK)
High-quality, shiny fabric.

**discriminated
(dis-KRIH-mih-nay-ted)**
Acted unfairly against, usually
based on religion or skin color.

duffels (DUH-fuls)
Lengths of coarse, heavy wool
fabric; often made into bags.

gallows (GAA-lows)
A structure used to hang
criminals.

Jew's harp
A small musical instrument held
against the teeth or lips, and
plucked with the fingers.

minister (MIH-nih-ster)
The leader of a non-Catholic,
Christian church.

saffron (SAA-fron)
Part of a dried flower used to
flavor food, in medicine, or as a
dye.

**sarsaparilla
(sas-puh-RIH-luh)**
Dried roots from the sarsaparilla
vine used in flavoring.

sassafras (SAA-suh-frass)
Dried root bark from the sassafras
tree used as a flavoring.

shanties
Primitive, poorly made structures
used for shelter.

wampum (WOM-pum)
Strings of polished beads used to
mark ceremonial occasions or as
trading goods.

Index